Easy Piano Selections

WEST SIDE STORY®

Based on a conception of Jerome Robbins

Book by
Arthur Laurents

Music by
Leonard Bernstein®

Lyrics by
Stephen Sondheim

Entire original production
directed and choreographed by
Jerome Robbins

ISBN 978-0-634-05184-5

LEONARD
BERNSTEIN
Music Publishing
Company LLC

BOOSEY & HAWKES

HAL•LEONARD®
CORPORATION
7777 W. BLUEMOUND RD. P.O. BOX 13819 MILWAUKEE, WI 53213

Visit Hal Leonard Online at **www.halleonard.com**

CONTENTS

ABOUT WEST SIDE STORY

In 1985, the authors of West Side Story came together at a Dramatists Guild Landmark Symposium to discuss their work. Terrence McNally acted as Moderator. The transcript of the entire session was published in the Dramatists Guild Quarterly (Autumn 1985). In the following excerpts, Jerome Robbins and Leonard Bernstein discuss the origin of the show and the collaboration that produced it.

TERRENCE McNALLY: It's hard to imagine what the musical theater would be like in 1985 without the efforts of the four gentlemen sitting here with me, the authors of *West Side Story*. In our theater community, they are held in great, great respect and much love. *West Side Story* is the one time these four extraordinary talents came together. I'd like to start with the germ of the idea, the first time somebody said, "Hey, there's a musical there," up through opening night in New York, in this case September 26, 1957, when *West Side Story* opened at the Winter Garden Theater.

JEROME ROBBINS: I don't remember the exact date – it was somewhere around 1949 – a friend of mine was offered the role of Romeo. He said to me, "This part seems very passive, would you tell me what you think I should do with it." I tried to imagine it in terms of today. That clicked in, and I said to myself, "There's a wonderful idea here." So I wrote a very brief outline and started looking for a producer and collaborators who'd be interested. This was not easy. Producers were not at all interested in doing it. Arthur and Lenny were interested, but not in getting together to work on it at that time, so we put it away. Many years later, they were involved in another musical and asked me to join them. I was not interested in *their* musical, but I did manage to say, "How about *Romeo and Juliet?*" I won them back to the subject, and that started our collaboration.

McNALLY: Were Arthur and Lenny the first librettist and composer you approached?

ROBBINS: Oh, yes. During the long period we put the project aside, I wasn't actively seeking other collaborators, I thought these were the best people for the material. I stuck to trying to get these guys, and when they came back to me I had the bait to grab them. ...

McNALLY: Lenny, part of the *West Side Story* lore is that you intended to do the lyrics yourself. Is that true?

LEONARD BERNSTEIN: ...Yes, when we began I had – madly – undertaken to do the lyrics as well as the music. In 1955, I was also working on another show, *Candide*, and then the *West Side Story* music turned out to be extraordinarily balletic – which I was very happy about – and turned out to be a tremendously greater amount of music than I had expected, ballet music, symphonic music, developmental music. For those two reasons, I realized that I couldn't do all that music, plus the lyrics, and do them well. Arthur mentioned that he'd heard a young fellow named Stephen Sondheim sing some of his songs at a party. ... I freaked out when Steve came in and sang his songs. From that moment to this, we've been loving colleagues and friends. ...

ROBBINS: I'd like to talk a little bit about that period, because it was one of the most exciting I've ever had in the theater: the period of the collaboration, when we were feeding each other all the time. We would meet wherever we could, depending on our schedules. Arthur would come in with a scene, the others would say they could do a song on this material, I'd supply, "How about if we did this as a dance?" There was this wonderful, mutual exchange going on. We can talk here about details, "I did this, I did that," but the essence of it was what we gave to each other, took from each other, yielded to each other, surrendered, reworked, put back together again, all of those things. It was a very important and extraordinary time. The collaboration was most fruitful during that digestive period. I say that because we got turned down so much, and for so many reasons, that we kept going back to the script, or rather our play, saying, "That didn't work, I wonder why not, what didn't they like, let's take a look at it again."

I remember Richard Rodger's contribution. We had a death scene for Maria – she was going to commit suicide or something, as in Shakespeare. He said, "She's dead already, after this all happens to her." So the walls we hit were helpful to us in a way, sending us back for another look. I'm glad we didn't get *West Side Story* on right away. Between the time we thought of it and finally did it, we did an immense amount of work on it.

BERNSTEIN: Amen to that. This was one of the most extraordinary collaborations of my life, perhaps *the* most, in that very sense of our nourishing one another. There was a generosity on everybody's part that I've rarely seen in the theater. For example, the song "Something's Coming" was a very late comer. We realized we needed a character-introduction kind of song for Tony. There was a marvelous introductory page in the script that Arthur had written, a kind of monologue, the essence of which became the lyric for this song. We raped Arthur's playwriting. I've never seen anyone so encouraging, let alone generous, urging us, "Yes, take it, take it, make it a song."

AMERICA

Lyrics by Stephen Sondheim

Music by Leonard Bernstein
Arranged by Carol Klose

Moderately bright

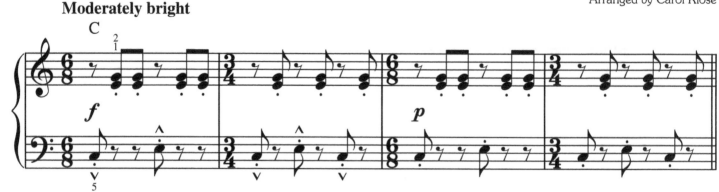

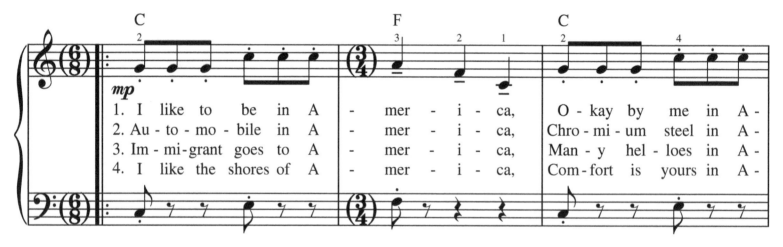

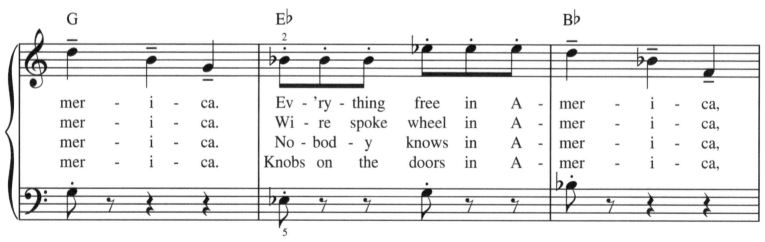

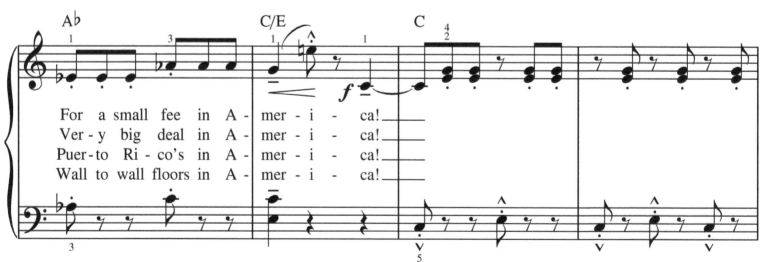

7

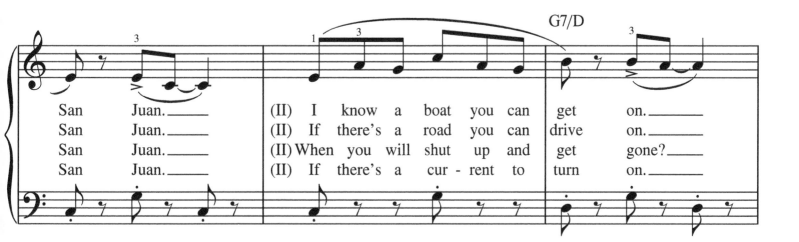

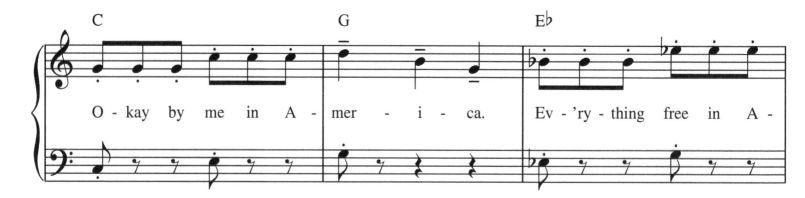

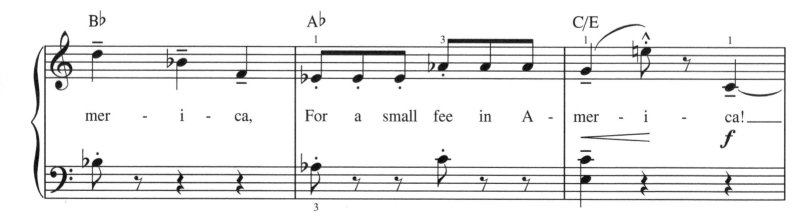

I FEEL PRETTY

Lyrics by Stephen Sondheim

Music by Leonard Bernstein
Arranged by Carol Klose

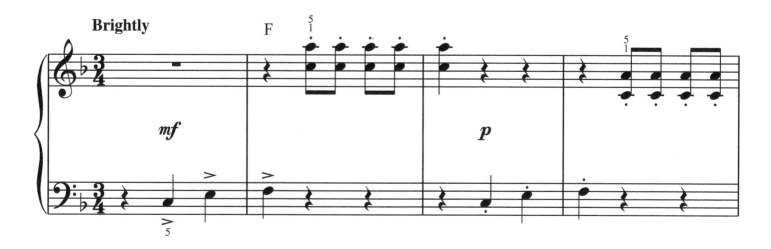

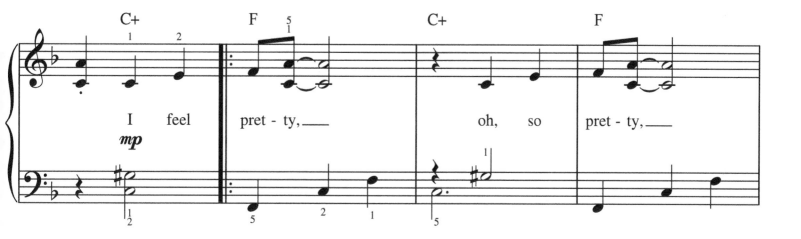

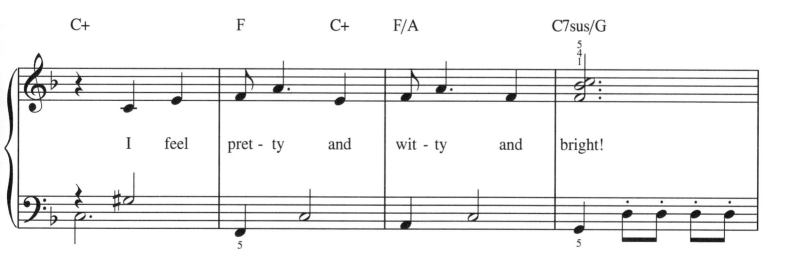

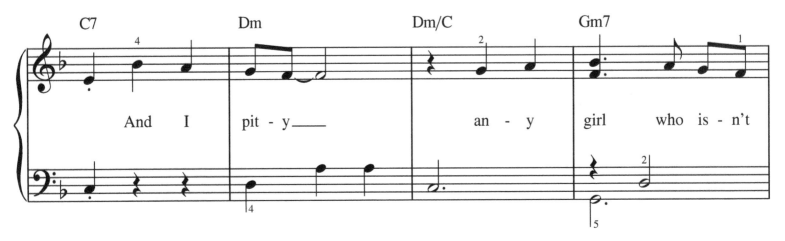

And I pit - y_____ an - y girl who is - n't

me to - night. I feel

I feel charm - ing,_____ oh, so

charm - ing,_____ it's a - larm - ing how charm - ing I

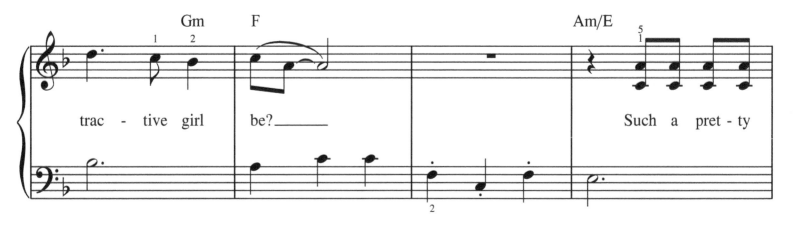

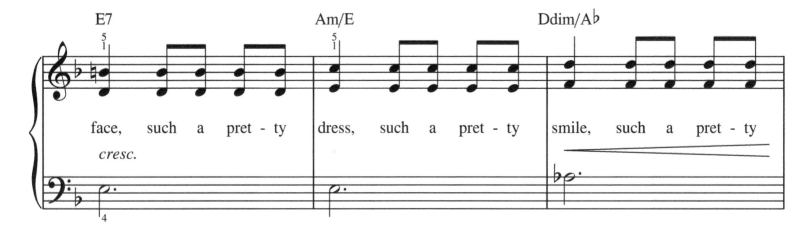

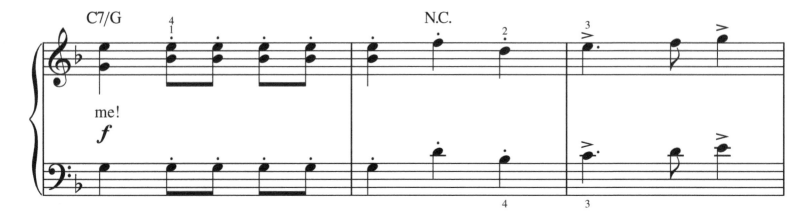

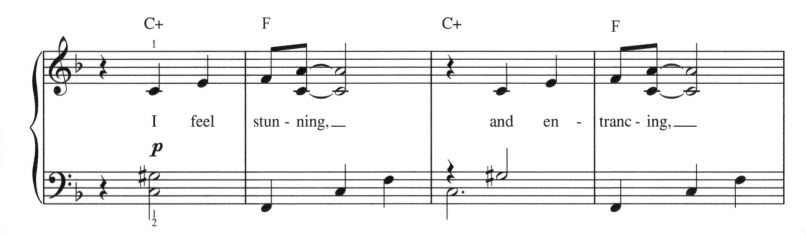

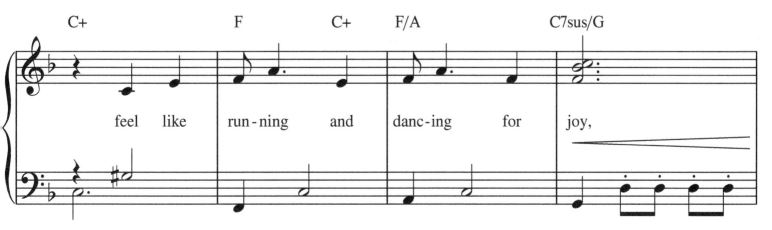

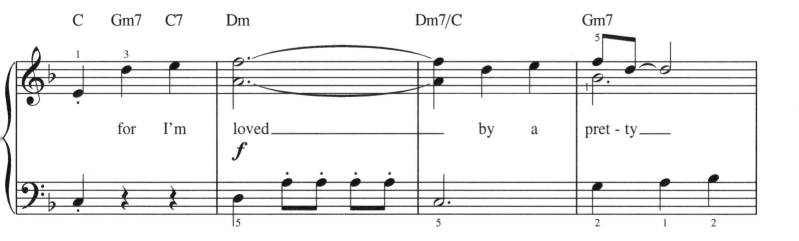

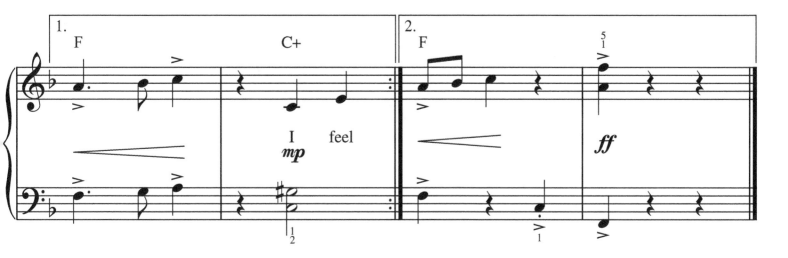

COOL

Lyrics by Stephen Sondheim

Music by Leonard Bernstein
Arranged by Carol Klose

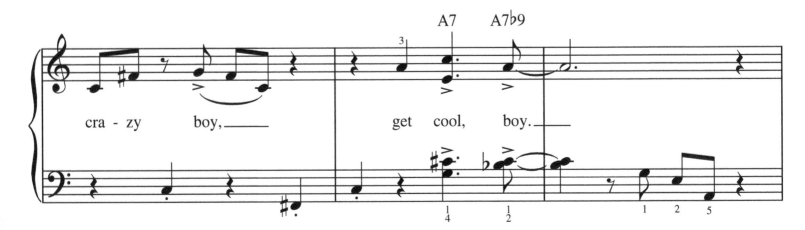

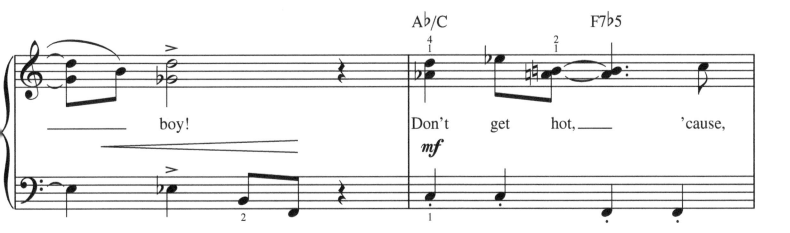

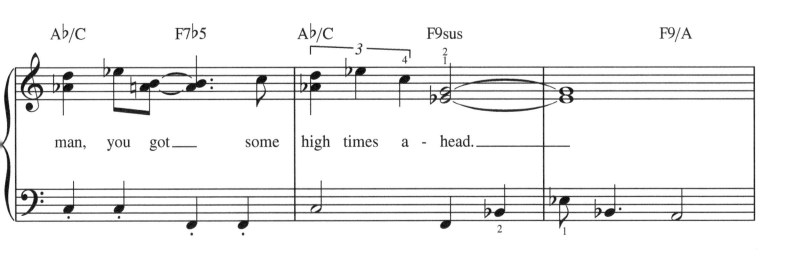

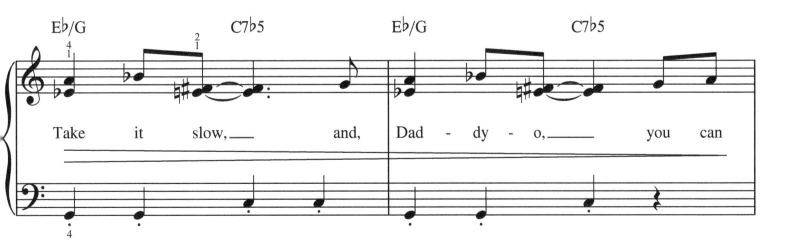

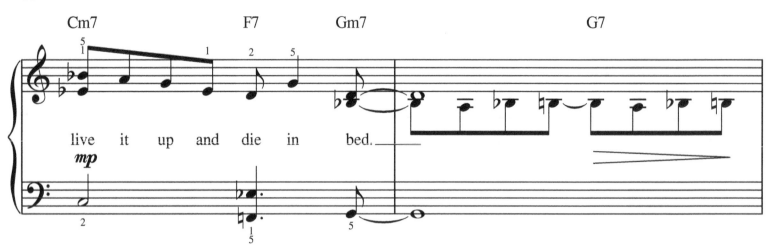

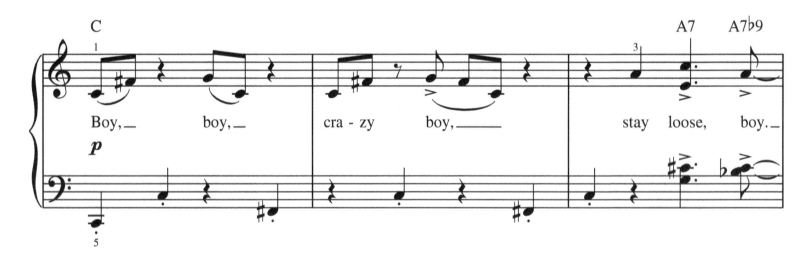

Go, man, go,___ but not like a yo - yo school boy,___

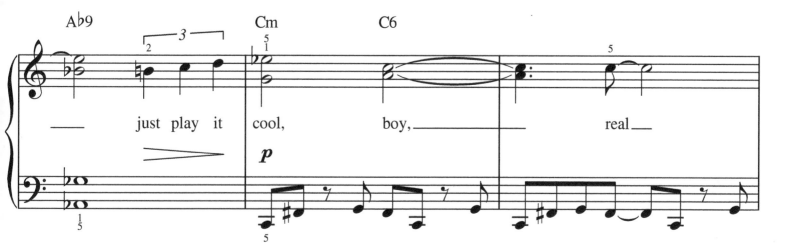

___ just play it cool, boy,_____ real___

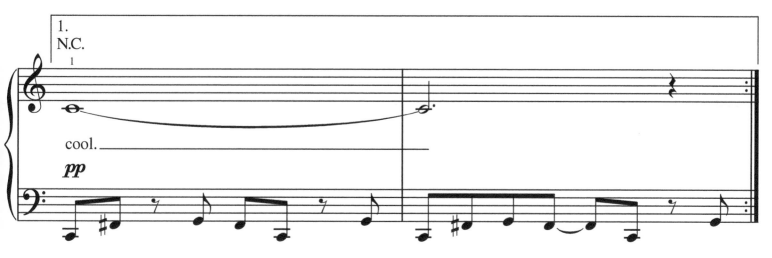

1.
N.C.

cool._____

2.
N.C.

cool._____

MARIA

Lyrics by Stephen Sondheim

Music by Leonard Bernstein
Arranged by Carol Klose

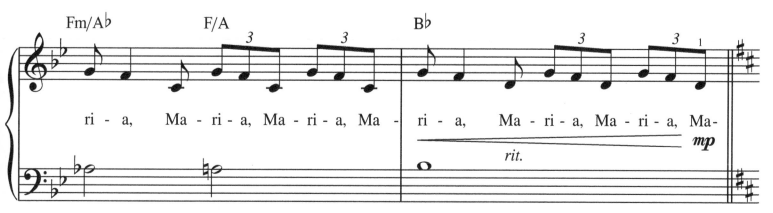

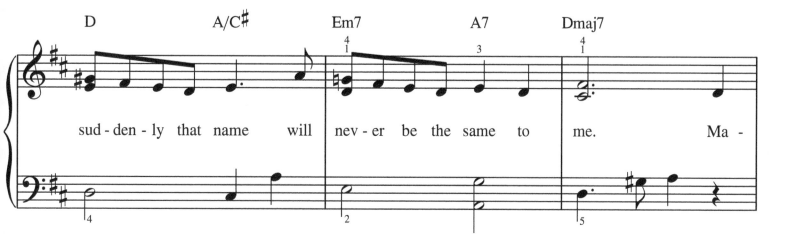

19

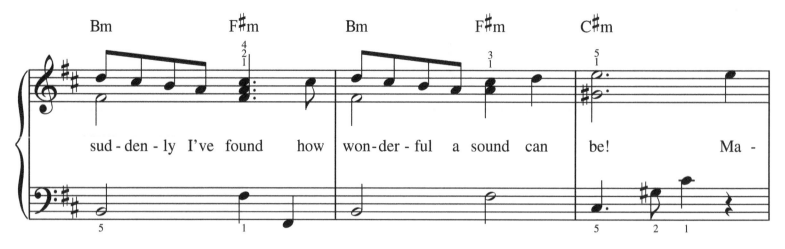

sud - den - ly I've found how won-der - ful a sound can be! Ma -

ri - a!_____ Say it loud and there's mu - sic play - ing. Say it
p

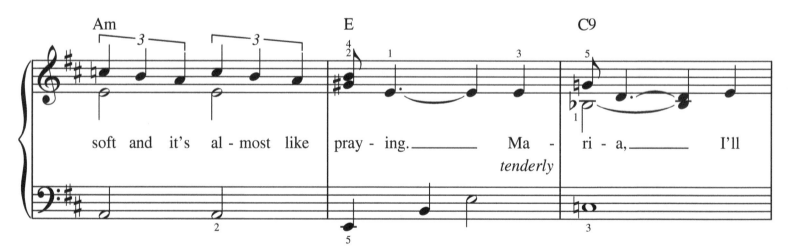

soft and it's al - most like pray - ing._____ Ma - ri - a,_____ I'll
tenderly

Slowly

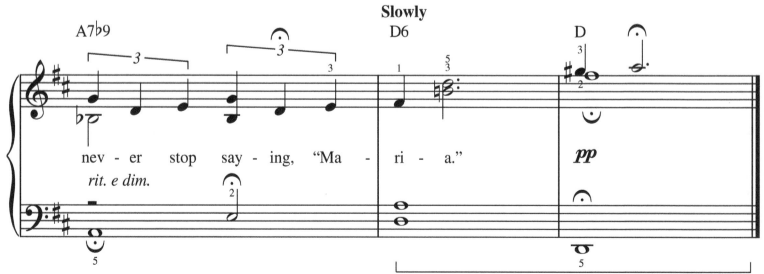

nev - er stop say - ing, "Ma - ri - a."
rit. e dim.
pp

ONE HAND, ONE HEART

Lyrics by Stephen Sondheim

Music by Leonard Bernstein
Arranged by Carol Klose

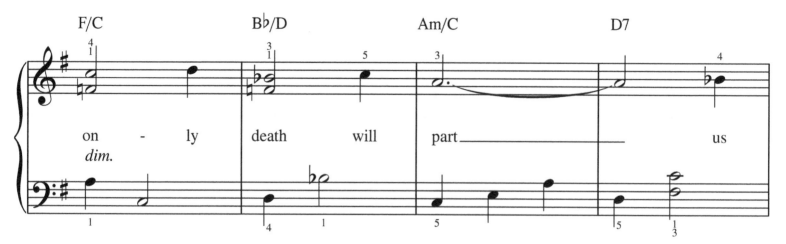

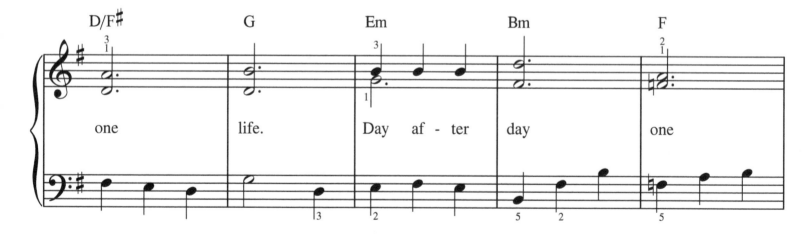

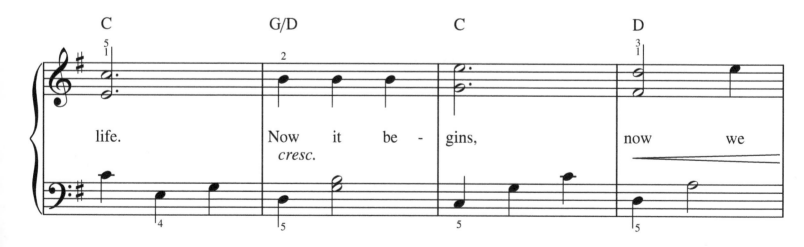

23

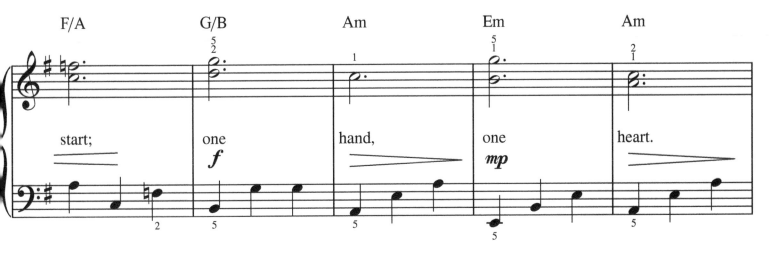

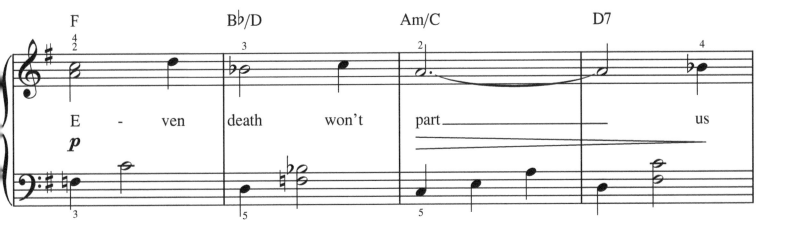

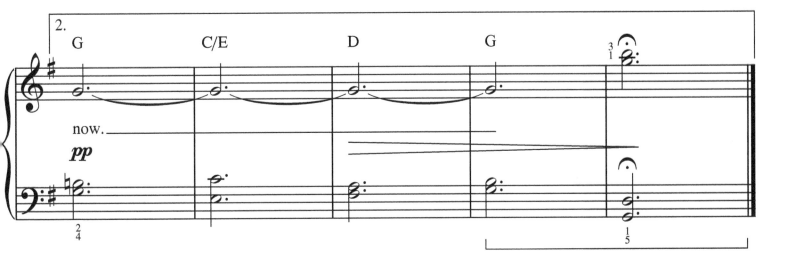

SOMETHING'S COMING

Lyrics by Stephen Sondheim

Music by Leonard Bernstein
Arranged by Carol Klose

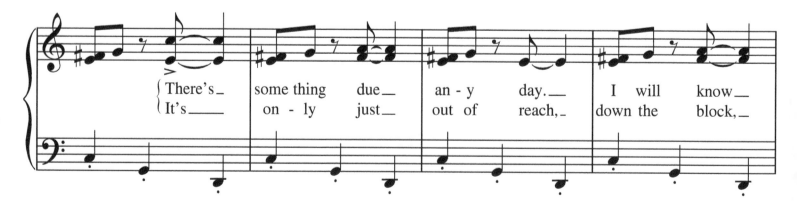

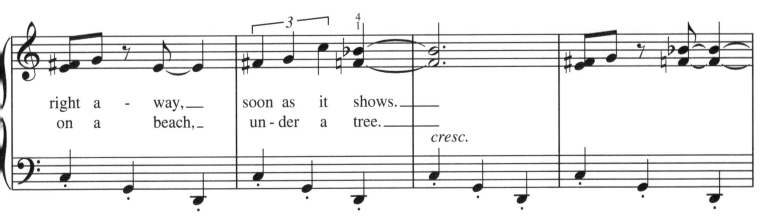

right a - way,__ soon as it shows.__
on a beach,_ un - der a tree.__

cresc.

Fmaj7   F13

f It may come can - non - ball - ing down thru the sky,
I got a feel - ing there's a mir - a - cle due,

Fmaj7   F13   1. Fmaj7

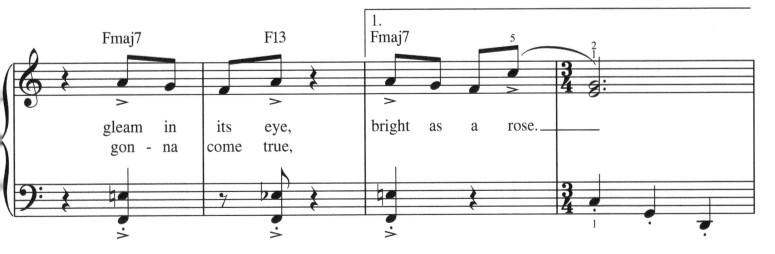

gleam in its eye, bright as a rose.__
gon - na come true,

2. Fmaj7

Who__ com - in' to me!__

p   *ff*

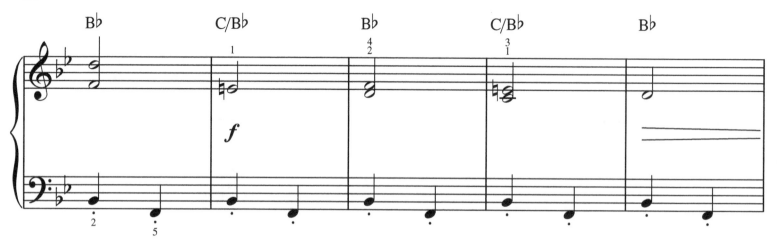

Refrain

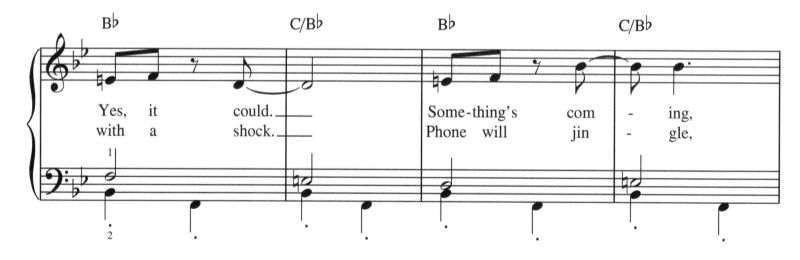

Could it be?_____
With a click,

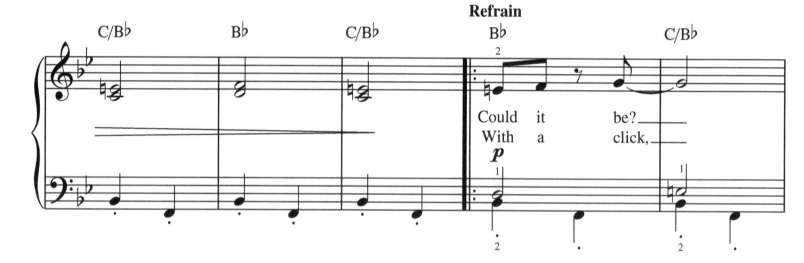

Yes, it could._____
with a shock._____

Some-thing's com - ing,
Phone will jin - gle,

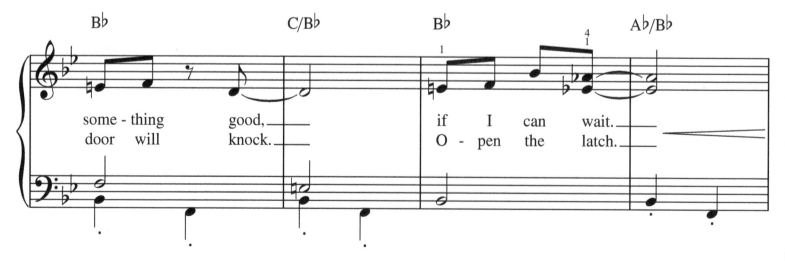

some - thing good,_____
door will knock._____

if I can wait._____
O - pen the latch._____

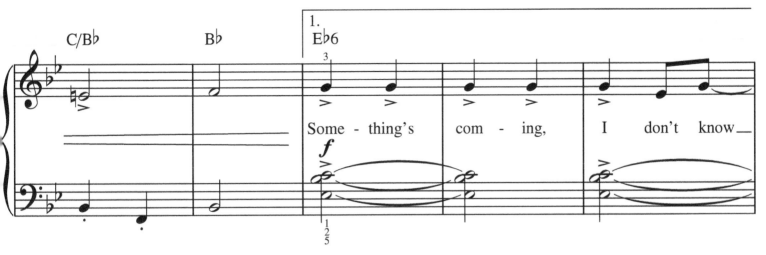

C/Bb   Bb   1. Eb6

Some - thing's com - ing, I don't know

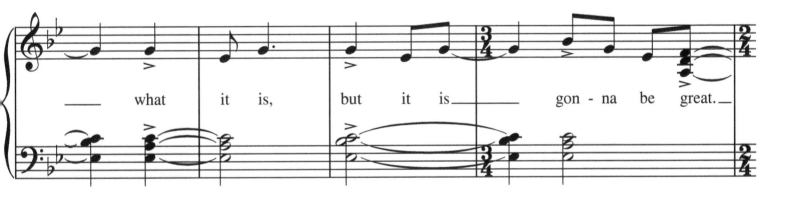

— what it is, but it is — gon - na be great. —

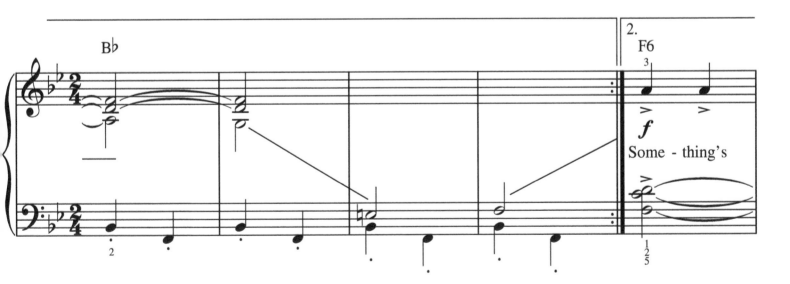

Bb   2. F6

Some - thing's

com - ing, don't know when — but it's soon;

catch the moon,_____ one - hand - ed catch.

Warmly

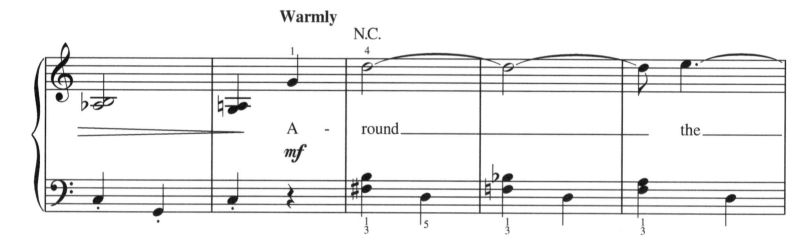

A - round_____ the_____

_____ cor - ner,_____ or

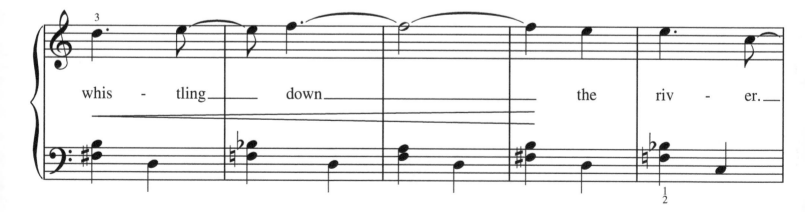

whis - tling_____ down_____ the riv - er.___

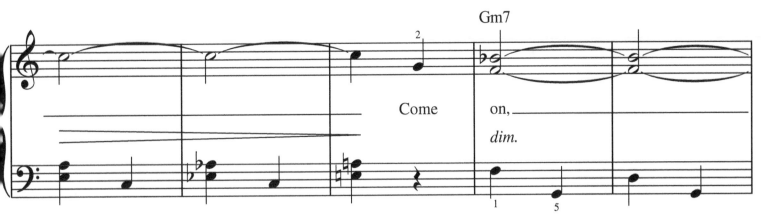

Come on,___

dim.

__ de - liv - er___

to me.___

p

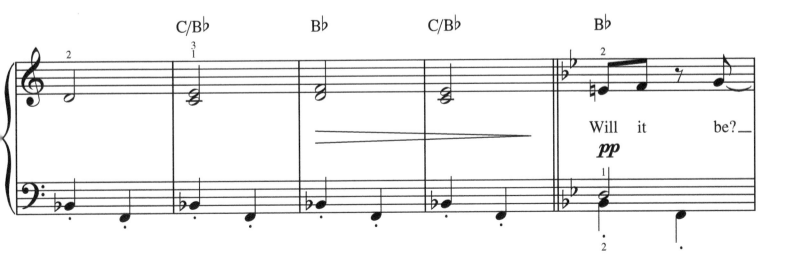

Will it be?___

pp

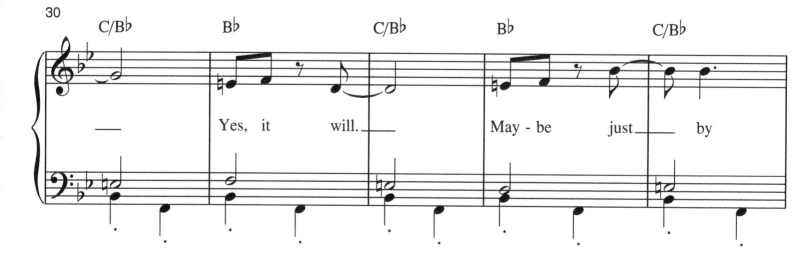

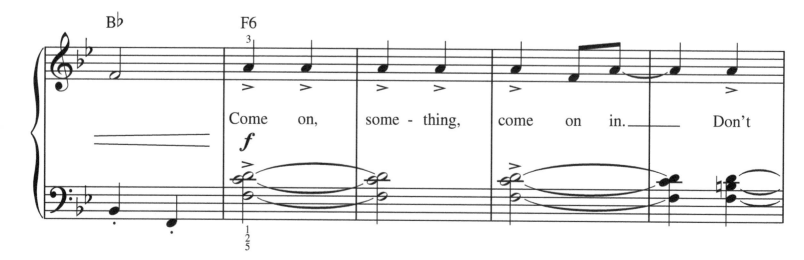

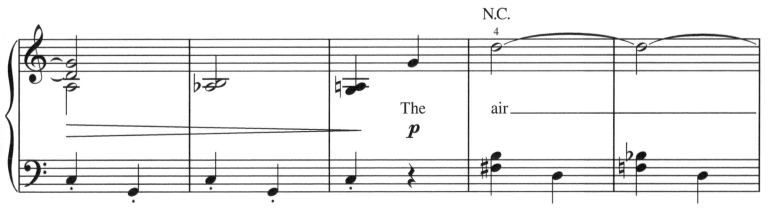

N.C.

The air

p

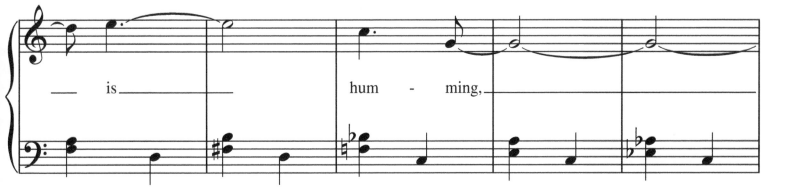

is   hum - ming,

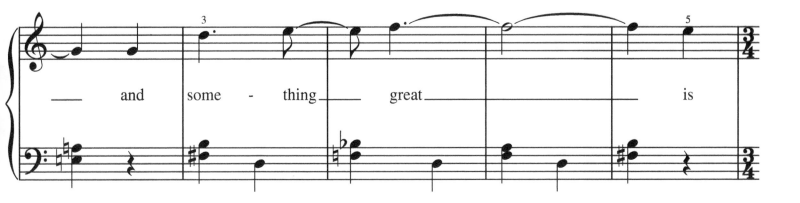

and some - thing great   is

com - ing. _   Who_ knows?_

It's — on - ly just —

out of reach, — down the block, — on a beach. — May-be to - night...

dim.

pp

ppp

TONIGHT

Lyrics by Stephen Sondheim

Music by Leonard Bernstein
Arranged by Carol Klose

Moderate Beguine tempo

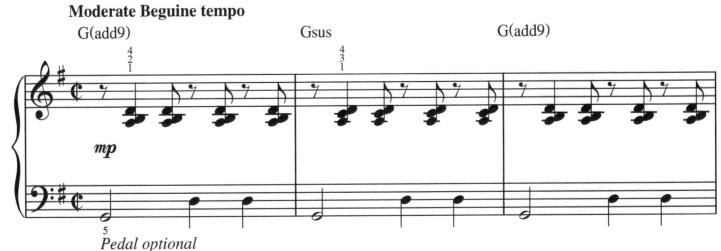

Pedal optional

To - night, to - night, won't

be just an - y night. To - night there will be

no morn - ing star. To -

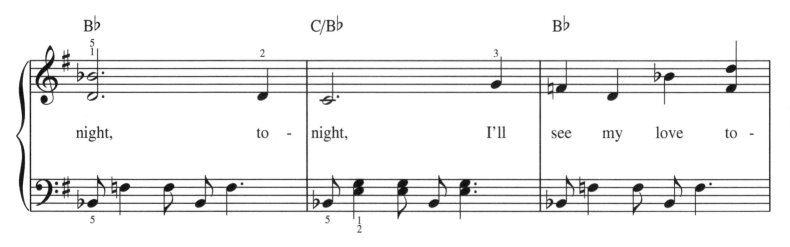

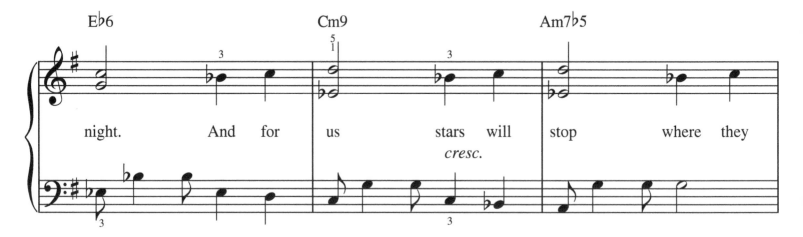

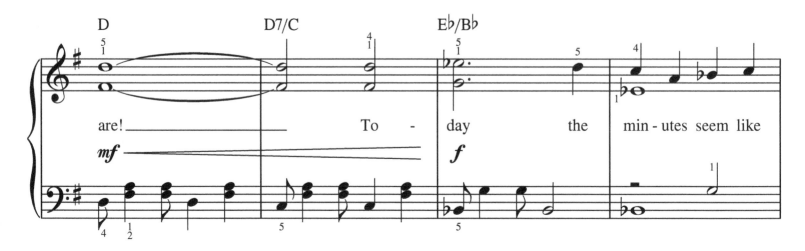

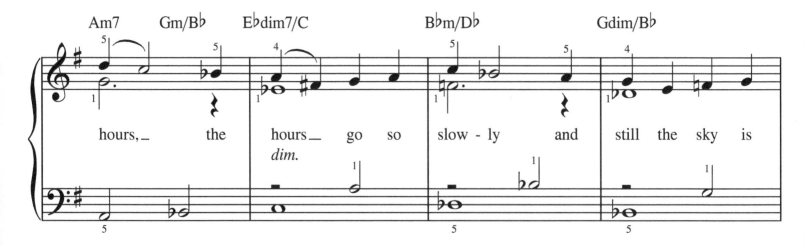

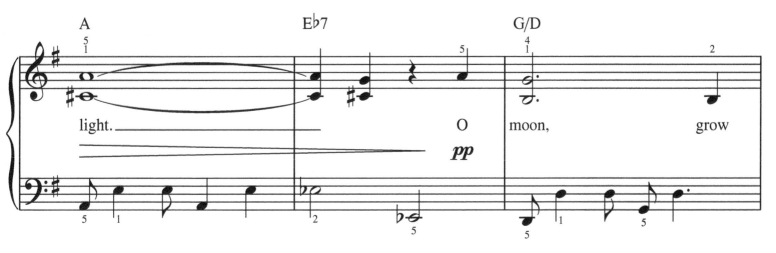

light. _____ O moon, grow

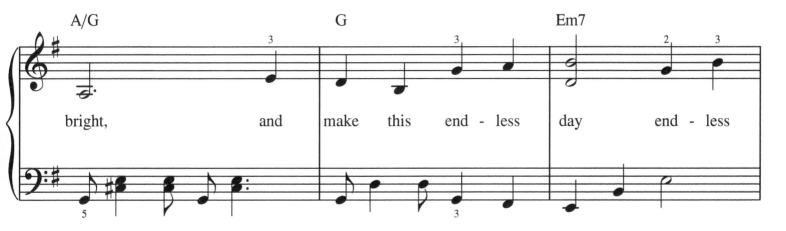

bright, and make this end - less day end - less

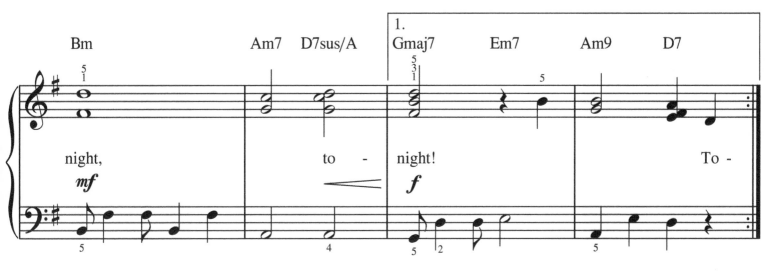

night, to - night! To -

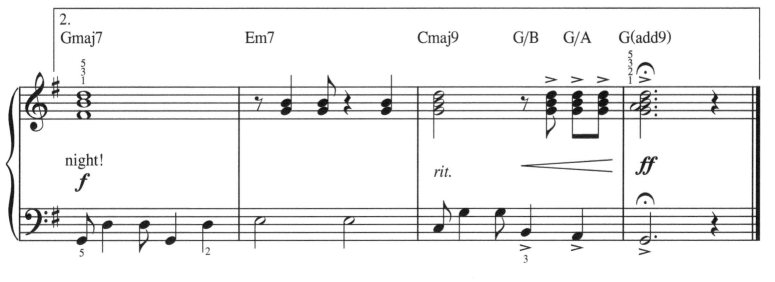

night!

SOMEWHERE

Lyrics by Stephen Sondheim

Music by Leonard Bernstein
Arranged by Carol Klose

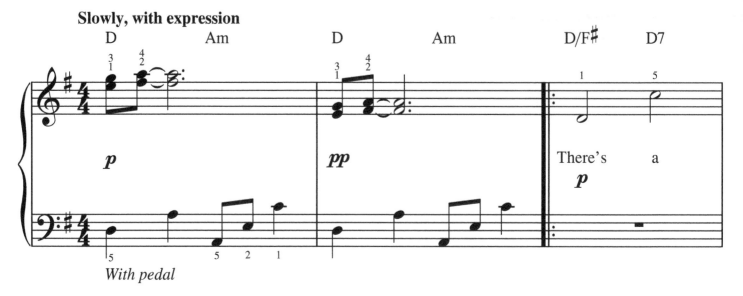

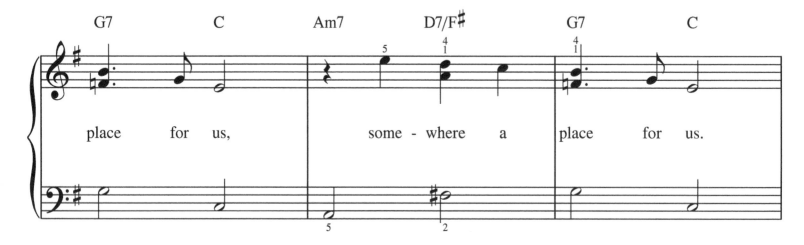

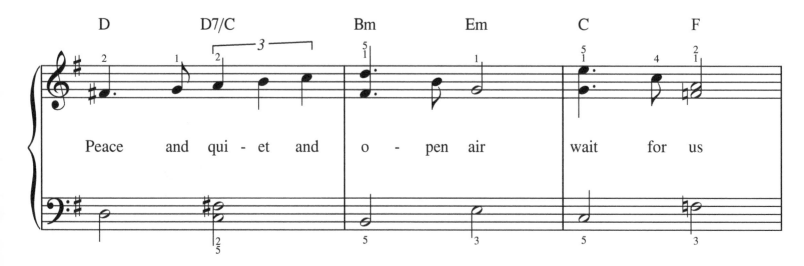

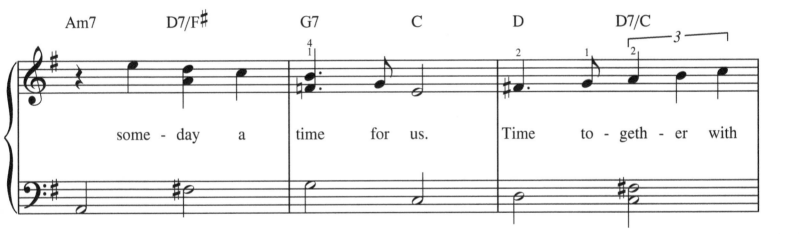

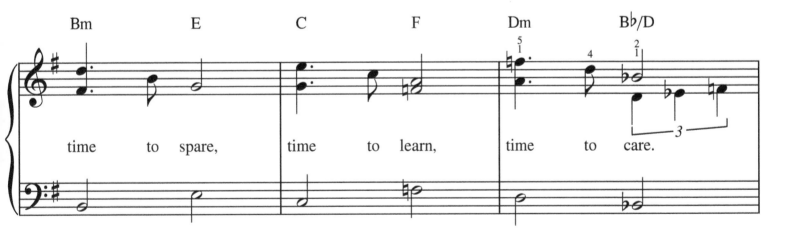

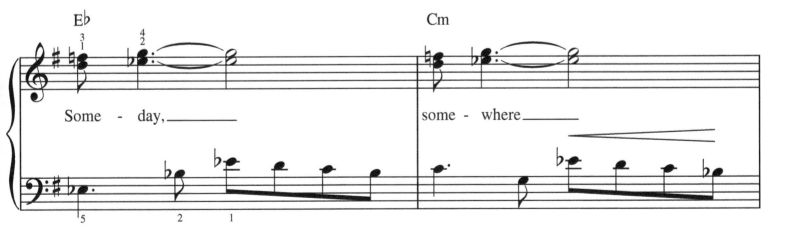

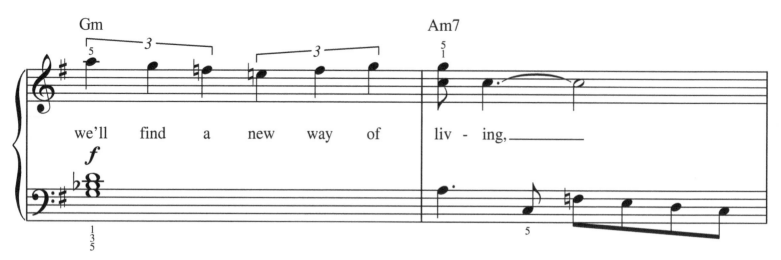

we'll find a new way of liv - ing,_____

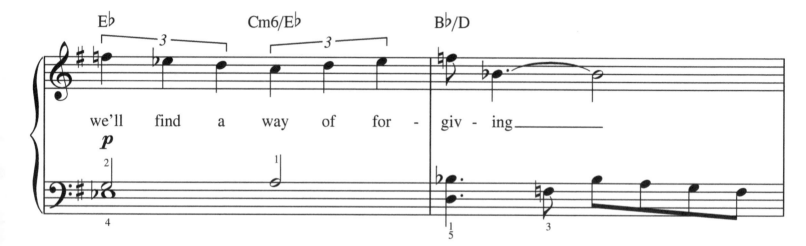

we'll find a way of for - giv - ing_____

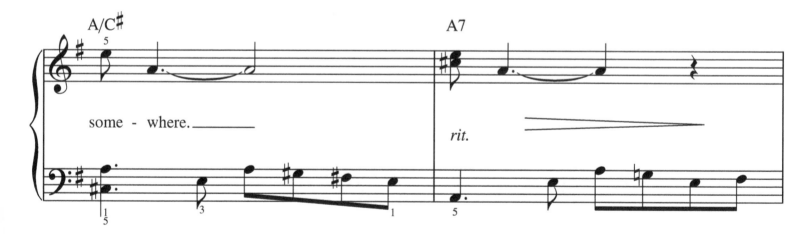

some - where._____

rit.

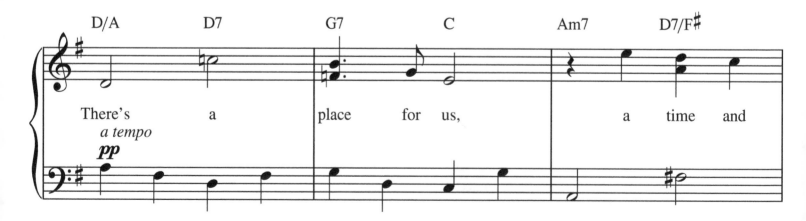

There's a place for us, a time and

a tempo

place for us. Hold my hand and we're half - way there.

Hold my hand and I'll take you there, some - how,____

cresc.

f

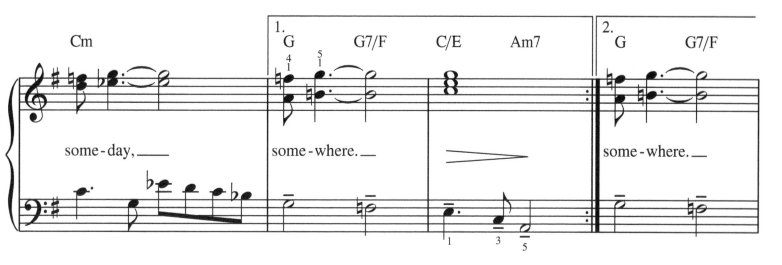

some - day,____ some - where.____ some - where.____

pp